LEVEL
1

Trot, Pony!

Shira Evans

NATIONAL
GEOGRAPHIC

Washington, D.C.

Welsh mountain pony

Trot, pony!

These young ponies play.

They live in a field.

Exmoor ponies

Dartmoor ponies

These ponies live
on a moor.

It's grassy and hilly here.

Ponies live in a group called a herd.

Icelandic horses

This herd lives near
the mountains.

This herd lives at the beach.

Chincoteague ponies

There are ponies with light hair.

Welsh pony

Exmoor pony

There are ponies with
dark hair.

Some ponies have short hair.

Haflinger pony

Shetland pony

Some ponies have
long hair.

All ponies eat grass.

Norwegian fjord horse

Welsh pony

They eat hay, too.

Shetland ponies

Play, ponies!

Trot, pony!

Shetland pony

Kinds of Ponies

There are many kinds of ponies. These are the kinds in this book.

ICELANDIC
HORSE

WELSH
MOUNTAIN PONY

EXMOOR
PONY

DARTMOOR
PONY

CHINCOTEAGUE
PONY

WELSH
PONY

HAFLINGER
PONY

SHETLAND
PONY

NORWEGIAN
FJORD HORSE

Draw a pony! Say what it looks like.

light hair
dark hair
short hair
long hair

This British English edition published in 2017 by Collins, an imprint of HarperCollins*Publishers*, The News Building, 1 London Bridge Street, London. SE1 9GF.

Browse the complete Collins catalogue at
www.collins.co.uk

A catalogue record for this publication is available from the British Library.

ISBN: 978-0-00-826653-0
US Edition ISBN: 978-1-4263-2413-0

Printed and bound in China by
RR Donnelley APS

The publisher gratefully acknowledges the expert literacy review of this book by Susan B. Neuman, Ph.D., professor of early childhood and literacy education, New York University.

Designed by Callie Broaddus

Photo Credits
Cover, Juniors Bildarchiv GmbH/Alamy; 1 (CTR), Juniors Bildarchiv GmbH/Alamy; 2-3 (CTR), Juniors Bildarchiv GmbH/Alamy; 4-5 (CTR), Wildlife GmbH/Alamy; 6-7 (CTR), David Lyons/Alamy; 8-9 (CTR), Ratnakorn Piyasirisorost/Getty Images; 10-11 (CTR), Stephen Bonk/Shutterstock; 12 (CTR), Juniors Bildarchiv GmbH/Alamy; 13 (CTR), Adam Burton/robertharding/Corbis; 14 (CTR), Katho Menden/Shutterstock; 15 (CTR), Juniors Bildarchiv GmbH/Alamy; 16 (CTR), Foto Grebler/Alamy; 17 (CTR), Groomes Photography/Getty Images; 18-19 (CTR), Juniors Bildarchiv GmbH/Alamy; 20-21 (CTR), Sabine Stuewer/KimballStock; 22 (UP LE), kb-photodesign/Shutterstock; 22 (CTR LE), Nicole Ciscato/Shutterstock; 22 (LO LE), Peak District Ventures/Getty Images; 22 (UP CTR), Zuzule/Shutterstock; 22 (CTR), Robert Kirk/Getty Images; 22 (LO CTR), David & Micha Sheldon/Getty Images; 22 (UP RT), Mike Charles/Shutterstock; 22 (CTR RT), Martyn Barnwell/Alamy; 22 (LO RT), David Robertson/Alamy; 23 (UP RT), Bogdan Ionescu/Shutterstock; 23 (CTR), Kaya Dengel; 23 (LO LE), Lukas Gojda/Shutterstock; 24 (UP), Juniors Bildarchiv GmbH/Alamy